# Words of Wisdom

# Innovators

## Also by Woody Woodward

*Millionaire Dropouts*
*Inspiring Stories of the World's Most Successful Dropouts*

*Millionaire Dropouts High School Edition*
*Never Let Your Schooling Interfere with Your Education*

*Millionaire Dropouts College Edition*
*Why Dropping Out Might Be the Best Decision You Ever Made*

*Millionaire Dropouts Parents Edition*
*Why You Should Support Your Child Who Wants to Drop Out*

*Millionaire Dropouts Biography Edition*
*Biographies of the World's Most Successful Failures*

*Millionaire Dropouts Mini-Book: Innovators*


## Also by Woody Woodward

*Millionaire Dropouts*
*Inspiring Stories of the World's Most Successful Dropouts*

*Millionaire Dropouts High School Edition*
*Never Let Your Schooling Interfere with Your Education*

*Millionaire Dropouts College Edition*
*Why Dropping Out Might Be the Best Decision You Ever Made*

*Millionaire Dropouts Parents Edition*
*Why You Should Support Your Child Who Wants to Drop Out*

*Millionaire Dropouts Biography Edition*
*Biographies of the World's Most Successful Failures*

*Millionaire Dropouts Mini-Book: Words of Wisdom*

# Millionaire Dropouts Mini-Book

# Words of Wisdom

## Woody Woodward

www.MillionaireDropouts.com

# Millionaire Dropouts Mini-Book

# Innovators

## Woody Woodward

www.MillionaireDropouts.com

© 2006 D.U. Publishing. All Rights Reserved.

Written permission must be secured from the publisher to use or reproduce any part of this book, except for brief quotations in critical reviews or articles. Request for permission or further information should be addressed to the Inspirational Product Division, D.U. Publishing.

D.U. Publishing
39252 Winchester Road #107-430
Murrieta CA 92563
admin@dupub.com
www.dupub.com

Millionaire Dropouts™ is trademark of Steven B. Woodward.

ISBN-10: 0-9785802-5-7
ISBN-13: 978-0-9785802-5-4

PRINTED IN USA

© 2006 D.U. Publishing. All Rights Reserved.

Written permission must be secured from the publisher to use or reproduce any part of this book, except for brief quotations in critical reviews or articles. Request for permission or further information should be addressed to the Inspirational Product Division, D.U. Publishing.

D.U. Publishing
39252 Winchester Road #107-430
Murrieta CA 92563
admin@dupub.com
www.dupub.com

Millionaire Dropouts™ is trademark of Steven B. Woodward.

ISBN-10: 0-9785802-6-5
ISBN-13: 978-0-9785802-6-1

PRINTED IN USA

# Dedication

To those whose passions cannot coexist with reality. Never let your schooling interfere with your education.

---

## Innovators

# Dedication

To those whose passions cannot coexist with reality. Never let your schooling interfere with your education.

## Contents

| | | | |
|---|---|---|---|
| 4 | Walt Disney | 34 | Earl Muntz |
| 6 | Thomas Edison | 36 | Isaac Singer |
| 8 | Amadeo Giannini | 38 | Wright Brothers |
| 10 | Wally Amos | 40 | David Copperfield |
| 12 | William Boeing | 42 | William Hanna |
| 14 | Soichiro Honda | 44 | Harry Houdini |
| 16 | Marcus Loew | 46 | Rosa Parks |
| 18 | Joseph Pulitzer | 48 | Sam Phillips |
| 20 | Frederick Royce | 50 | Andrew Lloyd Webber |
| 22 | Harland Sanders | 52 | Adolph Zukor |
| 24 | David Sarnoff | 54 | James Cameron |
| 26 | Vidal Sassoon | 56 | David Geffen |
| 28 | Dave Thomas | 58 | Wayne Huizenga |
| 30 | Kemmons Wilson | 60 | Steve Jobs |
| 32 | Florence Melton | 62 | Ray Kroc |

# Definition

**dropout:** 1. Anyone who gives up on an activity or goal. 2. Anyone who drops out of school or conventional society.

## Innovators

| | | | |
|---|---|---|---|
| 64 | Steven Spielberg | 100 | Richard Branson |
| 66 | John Astor | 102 | Bill Gates |
| 68 | Andrew Carnegie | 104 | John D. Rockefeller |
| 70 | Asa Candler | 106 | Christopher Columbus |
| 72 | Del Webb | 108 | Abraham Lincoln |
| 74 | Garrett Morgan | 110 | Benjamin Franklin |
| 76 | Edwin Land | 112 | George Washington |
| 78 | Elijah McCoy | 114 | Max Factor |
| 80 | Florence Graham | 116 | Ole Kirk Christian |
| 82 | Bill Rosenberg | 118 | Jackie Cochran |
| 84 | David Neelman | 120 | Valentina Tereshkova |
| 86 | Frank Mars | 122 | Berry Gordy |
| 88 | George Eastman | 124 | Frank Woodward |
| 90 | Hiroshi Yamauchi | 126 | Henry Ford |
| 92 | Horace Greeley | 128 | William Lear |
| 94 | Madame C.J. Walker | 130 | Nikola Tesla |
| 96 | Frank Lloyd Wright | 132 | Florence Nightingale |
| 98 | Hans Christian Andersen | 134 | William Shakespeare |

MILLIONAIRE DROPOUTS

# Definition

**dropout:** 1. Anyone who gives up on an activity or goal.
2. Anyone who drops out of school or conventional society.

www.MillionaireDropouts.com

# Words of Wisdom

## Innovators

# Introduction

Millionaire Dropouts started as a who's who of dropouts. Seven books later it has developed into an extensive list of great men and women who overcame their obstacles and succeeded in life. Some of the greatest companies and most important inventions began in the minds of people with very little education. How can someone without a degree and perhaps with very little money go on to build an empire? It is the age old question: What drives one person to succeed while another stops at failure? This book offers words of wisdom from some of the greatest dropouts in history. You may recognize a few; you may work for one of them. For a complete list of dropouts and bios of many of them, see the Millionaire Dropout series available at www.MillionaireDropouts.com.

# Introduction

Millionaire Dropouts started as a who's who of dropouts. Seven books later it has developed into an extensive list of great men and women who overcame their obstacles and succeeded in life. Some of the greatest companies and most important inventions began in the minds of people with very little education. How can someone without a degree and perhaps with very little money go on to build an empire? It is the age old question: What drives one person to succeed while another stops at failure? This book consists of bullet bios of some of the greatest dropouts in history. You may recognize a few, you may work for one of them. For a complete list of dropouts and additional bios, see the Millionaire Dropout series available at www.MillionaireDropouts.com.

Once in one's life, for one mortal moment,
one must make a grab for immortality; if not,
one has not lived.

—*Sylvester Stallone, actor*

Imagination is more important than knowledge.

—*Albert Einstein, physicist*

You don't take a photograph, you make it.

—*Ansel Adams, photographer*

# Walt Disney

**High School Dropout**

## Words of Wisdom

Obstacles are those frightful things you see when you take your eyes off your goal.
—*Henry Ford, founder, Ford Motor Company*

A day without laughter is a day wasted.
—*Charlie Chaplin, actor, silent films*

## Innovators

- Designed Mickey Mouse on a train ride after having his other cartoons rejected.
- Tried to get his best friend Art Linkletter to buy the orange groves around what would become Disneyland.
- Cashed in his life insurance policy to fund the start of Disneyland.
- Had his entire staff pirated from him by a competitor.
- Died of cancer before finishing his masterpiece, Walt Disney World.

Classes were always a bore to me. I wanted to learn things on my own, not by presentations. I was a loudmouth and a clown. It came as a surprise to me, later, that I could be serious and still get attention.

—*Nicolas Cage, actor*

# Thomas Edison

**Elementary School Dropout**

## Words of Wisdom

I think Hollywood has a class system. The actors are like the inmates, but the truth is they're running the asylum.

—*Robert De Niro, actor*

## Innovators

- Tried over 2,000 times to develop the incandescent light bulb.
- Sold his first invention for $40,000 in 1869, at the age of 22.
- While working on a new invention, lost his laboratory to a fire that burned it to the ground.
- Once employed fellow dropout Henry Ford.
- Actually bought a light bulb patent from James Woodward in 1879.

As a teenager I was so insecure. I was the type of guy that never fitted in because he never dared to choose. I was convinced I had absolutely no talent at all. And that thought took away all my ambition, too.

—*Johnny Depp, actor*

# Amadeo Giannini

**High School Dropout**

## Words of Wisdom

To be happy in this world, first you need a cell phone and then you need an airplane. Then you're truly wireless.

—*Ted Turner, billionaire, media*

I'm in no hurry to get anywhere. I don't have any plans. I don't have a map. If you did in this business, you'd destroy yourself.

—*Colin Farrell, actor*

## Innovators

- Founded the Bank of America.
- Sold his produce business in his thirties and could have retired, but went on to form his banking empire.
- Ran into his bank after the San Francisco earthquake in 1906, gathered all the gold and cash and set up a counter outside on the corner by putting a wood plank over two barrels.
- Started the first statewide banking system in the U.S.

Don't think for a moment that I'm really like any of the characters I've played. I'm not. That's why it's called "acting."

—*Leonardo DiCaprio, actor*

Family is not an important thing, it's everything.

—*Michael J. Fox, actor*

# Wally Amos

**High School Dropout**

## Words of Wisdom

She still talks to me now, only now she talks to me in my dreams. And I can't wait to go to sleep tonight because we have a lot to talk about. I love you.

—*Jamie Foxx, actor, referring to his grandmother when he won the Oscar for* Ray

I don't go by the rule book ... I lead from the heart, not the head.

—*Princess Diana, philanthropist*

## Innovators

- Founded Famous Amos Cookies.
- Attracted new talent, while working at the renowned William Morris Agency as a talent scout, by sending them cookies.
- Spent many years advancing the cause of adult literacy.
- Traveled the world as a motivational speaker.
- Is repesented in The Smithsonian Institution's Business Americana Collection by his famous Hawaiian shirt and battered banana hat.

A fool thinks himself to be wise, but a wise man knows himself to be a fool.
—*William Shakespeare, playwright*

Failure is a word that I simply don't accept.
—*John H. Johnson, founder,* Ebony Magazine

# William Boeing

**College Dropout**

## Words of Wisdom

I have found adventure in flying, in world travel, in business, and even close at hand ...
Adventure is a state of mind, and spirit.

—*Jacqueline Cochran, pilot*

Imagination is the beginning of creation.
You imagine what you desire, you will what you imagine and at last you create what you will.

—*George Bernard Shaw, playwright*

## Innovators

- Founded the Boeing Airplane Co.
- Dropped out of college the same year the Wright Brothers flew their first plane at Kitty Hawk.
- First made his fortune trading timber lands in the Seattle, Washington, area.
- Designed a twin-float seaplane as his first plane.
- Provided fifty planes to the U.S. Navy in World War I.

Pain is temporary, film is forever.
                                    —*Michael J. Fox*, actor

Make voyages! Attempt them ...
there's nothing else.
                                    —*Tennessee Williams*, playwright

If there is anything that a man can do well,
I say let him do it. Give him a chance.
                                    —*Abraham Lincoln*, president

# Soichiro Honda

**High School Dropout**

# Words of Wisdom

And while the law of competition may be sometimes hard for the individual, it is best for the race, because it ensures the survival of the fittest in every department.

—*Andrew Carnegie, millionaire*

Education is what remains after one has forgotten what one has learned in school.

—*Albert Einstein, physicist*

# Innovators

- Designed Honda motors and founded the Honda Motor Company.
- Sold his first company, a manufacturer of aircraft propellers, to Toyota, after World War II.
- Went on to develop an auxiliary motor for bicycles.
- Began developing motorcycle engines in 1948.
- Loved to race, until he had a terrible crash that left him with broken bones.
- Retired from racing at his wife's urging.

If I said to most of the people who auditioned,
"Good job, awesome, well done," it would have
made me actually look and feel ridiculous.
It's quite obvious most of the people
who turned up for this audition were hopeless.
—*Simon Cowell, producer*

# Marcus Loew

**Elementary School Dropout**

## Words of Wisdom

I don't believe that old cliché that good things come to those who wait. I think good things come to those who want something so bad they can't sit still.

—*Ashton Kutcher, actor*

Your worth consists in what you are and not in what you have.

—*Thomas A. Edison, inventor*

## Innovators

- Founded The Loews chain of movie theatres.
- Left elementary school in New York City when he was nine to help provide for his family.
- Formed MGM Studios with Louis B. Mayer and Samuel Goldwyn.
- Had 144 upscale movie houses by 1927.

Ability is of little account without opportunity.
—*Lucille Ball, actress*

In order to succeed, your desire for success should be greater than your fear of failure.
—*Bill Cosby, actor*

# Joseph Pulitzer

**High School Dropout**

## Words of Wisdom

I believe you make your day. You make your life. So much of it is all perception, and this is the form that I built for myself. I have to accept it and work within those compounds, and it's up to me.

—*Brad Pitt, actor*

All mankind is divided into three classes: those that are immovable, those that are movable, and those that move.

—*Benjamin Franklin, politician*

## Innovators

- Left Hungary at 17 and arrived in the U.S. penniless.
- Eventually got a job as a reporter for *Westliche Post*.
- Bought two competing newspapers and combined them into the *St. Louis Post-Dispatch*.
- Eventually bought the *World* from Jay Gould, who was losing money, and increased circulation to 600,000, making it the largest paper in the U.S.

A business has to be involving, it has to be fun, and it has to exercise your creative instincts.
—*Richard Branson, billionaire, VirginGroup*

A lot of talented actors still have to pay their bills.
—*Mark Wahlberg, actor*

# Frederick Royce

**Elementary School Dropout**

## Words of Wisdom

That's the trouble with being me. At this point, nobody gives a damn what my problem is. I could literally have a tumor on the side of my head and they'd be like, "Yeah, big deal. I'd eat a tumor every morning for the kinda money you're pulling down."

—*Jim Carrey, actor*

## Innovators

- Met his future partner Charles Rolls while Rolls was trying to find a replacement for his Panhard automobile.
- Designed and built the Rolls-Royce automobile.
- Developed the ultra-luxurious Silver Ghost with Rolls in 1906.
- Used technology developed for the the Silver Ghost to build reliable airplane engines for the army.

Quality means doing it right when no one is looking.

> —*Henry Ford, founder, Ford Motor Company*

Dear, never forget one little point. It's my business. You just work here.

> —*Florence Graham, founder, Elizabeth Arden*

I want to put a ding in the universe.

> —*Steve Jobs, billionaire, Apple Computer*

# Harland Sanders

**Middle School Dropout**

## Words of Wisdom

I think that gravity sets into everything, including careers, but pendulums do swing and mountains do become valleys after a while ... if you keep on walking.

*—Sylvester Stallone, actor*

I believe that everything happens for a reason, but I think it's important to seek out that reason— that's how we learn.

*—Drew Barrymore, actress*

## Innovators

- Lost his father when he was six and had to fend for himself in the kitchen while his mother worked.
- Dropped out of sixth grade to take a job for two dollars a month to help support his family.
- Didn't start making chicken to sell to people until he was in his forties.
- Started Kentucky Fried Chicken.
- Was made an honorary Colonel by Kentucky's governor in 1935.

The past cannot be changed. The future is yet in your power.

—*Mary Pickford, founder, United Artists*

Common sense is very uncommon.

—*Horace Greeley, founder, New York Tribune*

# David Sarnoff

**High School Dropout**

## Words of Wisdom

I find television very educating. Every time somebody turns on the set, I go into the other room and read a book.

—*Groucho Marx, comedian*

Too often I would hear men boast of the miles covered that day, rarely of what they had seen.

—*Louis L'Amour, author*

## Innovators

- Started working to help support his family at age nine.
- Left school at 15 to work full time.
- Promoted the idea of broadcasting, while at RCA, to give people a reason to purchase radios for their homes.
- Became general manager of RCA and founded the National Broadcast Company (NBC).
- Predicted TVs would replace radios.

But I am sure that I have always thought
of Christmas time, when it has come round …
as a good time; a kind, forgiving, charitable,
pleasant time; the only time I know of,
in the long calendar of the year, when men
and women seem by one consent to open their
shut-up hearts freely.

*—Charles Dickens, author*

# Vidal Sassoon

**Elementary School Dropout**

## Words of Wisdom

There is more treasure in books than in all the pirates' loot on Treasure Island and at the bottom of the Spanish Main … and best of all, you can enjoy these riches every day of your life.

—*Walt Disney, founder, The Walt Disney Company*

Hollywood is a place where they'll pay you a thousand dollars for a kiss and fifty cents for your soul.

—*Marilyn Monroe, actress*

## Innovators

- With his little brother, spent six years in an orphanage after their father stepped out on them when Vidal was only five.
- Wanted to be an architect but had to put his dreams on hold to work in a hair salon to support his family.
- Discovered his passion for fashion and style, charging up to $5,000 for a haircut.
- Founded Vidal Sassoon salon and hair care product companies.
- Owns and operates hair styling schools.

For me, ambition has become a dirty word.
I prefer hunger. To be hungry—great.
To have hopes, dreams—great.

*—Johnny Depp, actor*

I was not particularly bright, I wasn't very athletic, I was a little too tall, odd, funny looking, I was just really weird as a kid.

*—Uma Thurman, actress*

# Dave Thomas

**High School Dropout**

# Words of Wisdom

As we advance in life it becomes more and more difficult, but in fighting the difficulties the inmost strength of the heart is developed.

—*Vincent Van Gogh, artist*

## Innovators

- Was adopted when he was six weeks old and has financially supported and developed many adoption agencies nationwide.
- Got his start working for Colonel Sanders at KFC; took over their declining stores, turned them around and sold them back to Sanders for a handsome profit.
- Founded Wendy's Restaurants, named after his daughter.

Plastic surgery and breast implants are fine for people who want that, if it makes them feel better about who they are. But, it makes these people, actors especially, fantasy figures for a fantasy world. Acting is about being real being honest.

—*Kate Winslet, actress*

# Kemmons Wilson

**High School Dropout**

## Words of Wisdom

There are a lot of things that go into creating success. I don't like to do just the things I like to do. I like to do things that cause the company to succeed. I don't spend a lot of time doing my favorite activities.

—*Michael Dell, billionaire,
Dell Computer Corporation*

## Innovators

- Dropped out of school during the Great Depression to provide for his mother, who drilled into his head he could do anything he set his mind to.
- Set up a popcorn machine in a theater lobby and, by the age of 20, bought his first house.
- On vacation with his wife and kids, had to pay two dollars extra for each child, thought it was a rip-off and swore to start a hotel chain to provide better service.
- Founded the Holiday Inn hotel chain.

If you think you can do a thing or think you can't do a thing, you're right.
—*Henry Ford, founder, Ford Motor Company*

It's kind of fun to do the impossible.
—*Walt Disney, founder, The Walt Disney Company*

A day wasted on others is not wasted on one's self.
—*Charles Dickens, author*

# Florence Melton

**Elementary School Dropout**

## Words of Wisdom

Before everything else, getting ready is the secret of success.

—*Henry Ford, founder, Ford Motor Company*

Everybody likes to go their own way—to choose their own time and manner of devotion.

—*Jane Austen, author*

## Innovators

- While visiting the Firestone Tire and Rubber Company in Akron, Ohio, saw a piece of discarded latex and asked if she could have it.
- Went home and sewed on a soft cover to make a slipper and started selling a lot of them.
- Went into business with her husband and a partner, in 1947, when she was 36, to manufacture and sell her Angel Tread slippers.
- Grew the R.G. Barry Corp. to become the largest maker of comfort footwear in the world.

It's through curiosity and looking at opportunities in new ways that we've always mapped our path at Dell. There's always an opportunity to make a difference.

*—Michael Dell, billionaire,*
*Dell Computer Corporation*

Freedom is from within.

*—Frank Lloyd Wright, architect*

# Earl Muntz

**High School Dropout**

## Words of Wisdom

When I look in the mirror I see the girl I was when I was growing up, with braces, crooked teeth, a baby face and a skinny body.
—*Heather Locklear, actress*

I dream my painting, and then I paint my dream.
—*Vincent Van Gogh, artist*

If I only had a little humility, I'd be perfect.
—*Ted Turner, billionaire, media*

## Innovators

- Built his own radio at age 8 and one of the first car radios anywhere at age 14.
- Started selling used cars when he was 20 but had to have his mom do the paperwork because he was not of legal age.
- Was the first person to develop a black and white television set that sold for less than $200. Went bankrupt, losing millions, with the introduction of color television.
- Then invented the four-track car stereo that became an industry standard for two decades.

True artists, and I do think there are
some fashion-designer artists, create
because they can't do anything but create.
> —*Tom Ford, fashion designer*

I have sometimes been wildly, despairingly,
acutely miserable, racked with sorrow,
but through it all I still know quite certainly
that just to be alive is a grand thing.
> —*Agatha Christie, author*

# Isaac Singer

**Middle School Dropout**

## Words of Wisdom

I don't know the key to success, but the key to failure is trying to please everybody.

—*Bill Cosby, actor*

Do not copy my style! The first rule of writing is write about what you know, not what you think you know. So, think about what you've done in your life and write about that.

—*Jackie Collins, author*

## Innovators

- Invented a better sewing machine.
- Did not receive his patent for the improvement of sewing machines until he was 40, in 1851.
- Pooled his patents with those of other sewing machine manufactures rather than engage in a costly legal battle.
- Brought affordable and convenient sewing machines to homes around the world through innovative purchase plans and worldwide manufacturing.

You know what your problem is, it's that you haven't seen enough movies, all of life's riddles are answered in the movies.

—*Steve Martin, actor*

Credit is a system whereby a person who can not pay gets another person who can not pay to guarantee that he can pay.

—*Charles Dickens, author*

# Wright Brothers

**High School Dropouts**

## Words of Wisdom

I didn't go to high school, and I didn't go to grade school either. Education, I think, is for refinement and is probably a liability.
—*H. L. Hunt, billionaire, oil industry*

If you're not a risk taker, you should get the hell out of business.
—*Ray Kroc, billionaire, McDonald's Corporation*

## Innovators

- Started out with a bicycle repair shop.
- Tested and corrected published and accepted scientific data.
- Methodically analyzed and solved one engineering challenge after another.
- Succeeded, on December 17, 1903, at 10:35 AM, with Orville Wright at the controls, in the first controlled, machine-powered, sustained flight, lasting 12 seconds, launching the age of air travel as we know it.

All my life people have said that I wasn't going to make it.

— *Ted Turner, billionaire, media*

A man's moral conscience is the curse he had to accept from the gods in order to gain from them the right to dream.

— *William Faulkner, author*

# David Copperfield

**College Dropout**

## Words of Wisdom

I had no ambition to make a fortune.
Mere money-making has never been my goal,
I had an ambition to build.

—*John D. Rockefeller, billionaire, Standard Oil*

Be a yardstick of quality. Some people aren't used to an environment where excellence is expected.

—*Steve Jobs, billionaire, Apple Computer*

## Innovators

- Made the Statue of Liberty disappear.
- Walked through the Great Wall of China.
- Escaped from Alcatraz.
- Regularly selects 13 people at random from his audience and makes them disappear.
- Developed a rehabilitation program that uses sleight-of-hand magic to improve dexterity and motor skills, a program now used in over 1,000 hospitals in 30 countries.

A gentleman can live through anything.
—*William Faulkner,* author

The thing women have yet to learn
is nobody gives you power. You just take it.
—*Roseanne Barr,* actress

# William Hanna

**College Dropout**

## Words of Wisdom

Knowledge is like money: to be of value it must circulate, and in circulating it can increase in quantity and, hopefully, in value.

—*Louis L'Amour, author*

Charity is injurious unless it helps the recipient to become independent of it.

—*John D. Rockefeller, billionaire, Standard Oil*

## Innovators

- Formed Hanna–Barbera Productions with his co-worker Joseph Barbera when MGM closed down their animation department.
- Wrote and illustrated the popular *Tom and Jerry* cartoon series.
- Created *The Flintstones*, the first half-hour animated sitcom on television.
- Createed other popular characters, including Huckleberry Hound, Yogi Bear, Johnny Quest, Banana Splits, and Scooby Doo.

Great things are done by a series of small things brought together.

—*Vincent Van Gogh, artist*

What should exist? To me, that's the most exciting question imaginable. What do we need that we don't have? How can we realize our potential?

—*Paul Allen, billionaire, Microsoft*

# Harry Houdini

**Elementary School Dropout**

## Words of Wisdom

I am looking for a lot of men who have an infinite capacity to not know what can't be done.
—*Henry Ford, founder, Ford Motor Company*

## Innovators

- Changed his name to Houdini because his idol was French magician Robert Houdin.
- Got his start performing, at 17, in amusement parks and dime museums.
- Became famous for escaping from handcuffs provided by the local police when he toured and for the Chinese water torture cell.
- Traveled the country in 1920 exposing psychics and mediums for their deceptive practices.

I believe in the dignity of labor, whether with head or hand; that the world owes no man a living but that it owes every man an opportunity to make a living.
—*John D. Rockefeller, billionaire, Standard Oil*

# Rosa Parks

**High School Dropout**

Ridiculous yachts and private planes and big limousines won't make people enjoy life more, and it sends out terrible messages to the people who work for them. It would be so much better if that money was spent in Africa, and it's about getting a balance.

—*Richard Branson, billionaire, Virgin Group*

## Innovators

- Changed the country when she would not give up her seat on the bus to a white man.
- Was arrested, tried and convicted for violating the local ordinance, triggering a boycott of city buses that lasted over a year.
- Was instrumental in Dr. Martin Luther King Jr.'s rise to prominence, thanks to his involvement in the boycott.

From the time we're born until we die,
we're kept busy with artificial stuff
that isn't important.

—*Tom Ford, fashion designer*

Always dream and shoot higher than you
know you can do. Don't bother just to be better
than your contemporaries or predecessors.
Try to be better than yourself.

—*William Faulkner, author*

# Sam Phillips

**High School Dropout**

## Words of Wisdom

You can't just ask customers what they want and then try to give that to them. By the time you get it built, they'll want something new.
—*Steve Jobs, billionaire, Apple Computer*

Conscience is a man's compass.
—*Vincent Van Gogh, artist*

## Innovators

- Dropped out of high school to take care of his mother and aunt.
- Founded Sun Records.
- Discovered Elvis Presley.
- Recorded artists including B.B. King, Johnny Cash, Jerry Lee Lewis, Roy Orbison and Carl Perkins.
- In 1955, fell on hard times and was forced to sell Elvis's lucrative contract to RCA records for $35,000.

One doesn't recognize the really important moments in one's life until it's too late.

—*Agatha Christie, author*

Anger is a killing thing: it kills the man who angers, for each rage leaves him less than he had been before—it takes something from him.

—*Louis L'Amour, author*

# Andrew Lloyd Webber

**College Dropout**

## Words of Wisdom

The number one benefit of information technology is that it empowers people to do what they want to do. It lets people be creative. It lets people be productive. It lets people learn things they didn't think they could learn before, and so in a sense it is all about potential.

—*Steve Ballmer, billionaire, Microsoft*

## Innovators

- Dropped out of college to write musicals with lyricist Tim Rice in 1964.
- Had their first success in 1968 with *Joseph and the Amazing Technicolor Dreamcoat*.
- Wrote *Cats*, which set the record for London and New York for the longest running musical, closing after 7,485 performances.
- In 1986, wrote *Phantom of the Opera*, which still plays worldwide.

Anybody who thinks money will make you happy hasn't got money.
—*David Geffen, billionaire, DreamWorks SKG*

# Adolph Zukor

**High School Dropout**

## Words of Wisdom

There are two fools in this world. One is the millionaire who thinks that by hoarding money he can somehow accumulate real power, and the other is the penniless reformer who thinks that if only he can take the money from one class and give it to another, all the world's ills will be cured.

—*Henry Ford, founder, Ford Motor Company*

## Innovators

- Started at 16 as a sweeper in a fur shop in New York City.
- Opened his own shop years later.
- Partnered with fellow dropout Marcus Loew, buying a chain of arcades.
- Started his own movie production company.
- Eventually purchased a company called Paramount Distribution, renamed it Paramount Pictures, which became the biggest studio in Hollywood.

Success is a lousy teacher. It seduces smart people into thinking they can't lose.

—*Bill Gates, billionaire, Microsoft*

Innovation distinguishes between a leader and a follower.

—*Steve Jobs, billionaire, Apple Computer*

# James Cameron

**College Dropout**

## Words of Wisdom

When you're the first person whose beliefs are different from what everyone else believes, you're basically saying, "I'm right, and everyone else is wrong." That's a very unpleasant position to be in. It's at once exhilarating and at the same time an invitation to be attacked.

—*Larry Ellison, billionaire, Oracle*

## Innovators

- Directed the highest grossing movie of all time, *Titanic*.
- Got his start at Roger Corman Studios as a model maker.
- Wrote and directed the *Terminator* movies based on a nightmare he had about a robot hit man sent from the future to kill him.

Victory is won not in miles but in inches. Win a little now, hold your ground, and later, win a little more.

—*Louis L'Amour, author*

Business opportunities are like buses, there's always another one coming.

—*Richard Branson, billionaire, Virgin Group*

# David Geffen

**College Dropout**

## Words of Wisdom

The secret of getting ahead is getting started.
—*Agatha Christie, author*

Decide what you want, decide what you are willing to exchange for it. Establish your priorities and go to work.
—*H. L. Hunt, billionaire, oil industry*

## Innovators

- Started his career as an usher at CBS-TV studios.
- Moved on to become a talent agent for the William Morris Agency.
- Started his own record label at 28, Asylum Records, which he sold within two years to Warner Bros.
- Was in his late thirties when he founded Geffen records, which he ended up selling within 10 years to MCA for an estimated $550 million.

Have a heart that never hardens, and a temper that never tires, and a touch that never hurts.
—*Charles Dickens, author*

I dream for a living.
—*Steven Spielberg, billionaire, DreamWorks SKG*

All our dreams can come true, if we have the courage to pursue them.
—*Walt Disney, The Walt Disney Company*

# Wayne Huizenga

**College Dropout**

## Words of Wisdom

I believe that man will not merely endure. He will prevail. He is immortal, not because he alone among creatures has an inexhaustible voice, but because he has a soul, a spirit capable of compassion and sacrifice and endurance.

—*William Faulkner, author*

You learn in this business: It you want a friend, get a dog.

—*Carl Icahn, billionaire, corporate raider*

## Innovators

- Got his start in the trash hauling business.
- Started buying smaller companies and competitors and in 1971 formed Waste Management Inc.
- Was so impressed after visiting a Blockbuster Video store that he bought the company.
- Expanded the Blockbuster franchise nationwide, becoming one of the most powerful people in the entertainment industry.

The darkest hour in any man's life is when he sits down to plan how to get money without earning it.
—*Horace Greeley, founder,* New York Tribune

Eighty percent of success is showing up.
—*Woody Allen, filmmaker*

I can't change the direction of the wind, but I can adjust my sails to always reach my destination.
—*Jimmy Dean, Jimmy Dean Foods*

# Steve Jobs

**College Dropout**

## Words of Wisdom

We didn't know how to run a business, but we had dreams and talent. I wasn't a financial pro, and I paid the price.

—*Ruth Handler, founder, Mattel*

To disbelieve is easy; to scoff is simple; to have faith is harder.

—*Louis L'Amour, author*

## Innovators

- Was adopted as an infant.
- Started Apple Computers in his parents' garage.
- Was fired from the company he founded.
- Went on to create the NeXT computer, which Apple Computer purchased in 1996 for $402 million, making Jobs CEO of Apple.
- Drove the development of the iPod.

Nothing is an obstacle unless you say it is.
—*Wally Amos, founder, Famous Amos Cookies*

Do not quench your inspiration and your imagination; do not become the slave of your model.
—*Vincent Van Gogh, artist*

# Ray Kroc

**High School Dropout**

## Words of Wisdom

It is astonishing what an effort it seems to be for many people to put their brains definitely and systematically to work.

*—Thomas A. Edison, inventor*

A person who never made a mistake never tried anything new.

*—Albert Einstein, physicist*

## Innovators

- Lied about his age, dropping out of high school, to join the Red Cross during World War I.
- Met the McDonald brothers while selling them Multimixers, then purchased their company for $2.7 million.
- Formed McDonald's Corporation and opened thousands of restaurants.
- Changed the world of fast food restaurants and the way people eat around the world.

I don't get high, but sometimes I wish I did. That way, when I messed up in life I would have an excuse. But right now there's no rehab for stupidity.

*—Chris Rock, comedian*

I believe in divine forces and energies.

*—Richard Pryor, comedian*

# Steven Spielberg

**College Dropout**

## Words of Wisdom

To turn really interesting ideas and fledgling technologies into a company that can continue to innovate for years, it requires a lot of disciplines.

—*Steve Jobs, billionaire, Apple Computer*

I think you have to judge everything based on your personal taste. And if that means being critical, so be it. I hate political correctness. I absolutely loathe it.

—*Simon Cowell, producer*

## Innovators

- Was rejected twice for the film course at the University of Southern California.
- Directed some of the best-loved movies of all time, including *Jurassic Park, Raiders of the Lost Ark, Saving Private Ryan, War of the Worlds* and the movie that made children everywhere afraid to go in the water, *Jaws*.
- Cofounded the first new major production company in decades, DreamWorks SKG.

A life spent making mistakes is not only more honorable but more useful than a life spent doing nothing.

—*George Bernard Shaw, playwright*

What's the quickest way to become a millionaire? Borrow fivers off everyone you meet.

—*Richard Branson, billionaire, Virgin Group*

# John Astor

**High School Dropout**

## Words of Wisdom

Why pay a dollar for a bookmark? Why not use the dollar for a bookmark?

—*Steven Spielberg, billionaire, DreamWorks SKG*

If you work just for money, you'll never make it, but if you love what you're doing and you always put the customer first, success will be yours.

—*Ray Kroc, billionaire, McDonald's Corporation*

## Innovators

- Left home at 16 to help in his brother's musical instrument business.
- Traveled to look for new avenues to sell musical instruments after the Revolutionary War.
- Learned of the high demand for fur at that time and opened his first fur shop before he turned 30.
- Turned his energies to real estate when the fur market declined.
- By his death he was the first millionaire in the U.S.

I believe that every right implies a responsibility;
every opportunity an obligation;
every possession a duty.

— *John D. Rockefeller, billionaire, Standard Oil*

I honestly think it is better to be a failure
at something you love than to be a success at
something you hate.

— *George Burns, comedian*

# Andrew Carnegie

**Elementary School Dropout**

## Words of Wisdom

I've never run into a guy who could win at the top level in anything today and didn't have the right attitude, didn't give it everything he had, at least while he was doing it; wasn't prepared and didn't have the whole program worked out.

—*Ted Turner, billionaire, media*

## Innovators

- Worked as a bobbin boy in a cotton factory for $1.20 a week, at 13, to help support his family.
- Partnered, years later, with the inventor of the sleeping car to sell the cars to the railroad where he then worked.
- Invested in steel factories in the 1890s and, by 1901, sold his holdings to J.P. Morgan for $480 million.
- Established over 1,600 libraries in the U.S.
- Gave away over $380 million before his death.

It's easy to have principles when you're rich. The important thing is to have principles when you're poor.

—*Ray Kroc, billionaire, McDonald's Corporation*

The quickest way to a man's heart is through his chest.

—*Roseanne Barr, comedian*

# Asa Candler

**College Dropout**

## Words of Wisdom

The difference between the impossible and the possible lies in a man's determination.

—*Tommy Lasorda, baseball manager*

I believe the ability to think is blessed. If you can think about a situation, you can deal with it. The big struggle is to keep your head Clear enough to think.

—*Richard Pryor, comedian*

## Innovators

- Purchased the recipe for Coca-Cola from the inventor, Dr. John Pembert, for $2,300.
- Made Coca-Cola the most requested soft drink on the market within two decades.
- Sold Coca-Cola for $25 million to Ernest Woodruff after Prohibition ended.

People discuss my art and pretend to understand as if it were necessary to understand, when it's simply necessary to love.
—*Claude Monet, artist*

A man is a fool if he drinks before he reaches the age of 50, and a fool if he doesn't afterward.
—*Frank Lloyd Wright, architect*

# Del Webb

**High School Dropout**

## Words of Wisdom

I believe in being an innovator.
—*Walt Disney, founder, The Walt Disney Company*

For the execution of the voyage to the Indies, I did not make use of intelligence, mathematics or maps.
—*Christopher Columbus, explorer*

My son is now an "entrepreneur." That's what you're called when you don't have a job.
—*Ted Turner, billionaire, media*

## Innovators

- Left high school to work and support the family when his wealthy father went bankrupt.
- Set up a small construction business at 29.
- Did well in the post–World War II housing boom.
- Purchased the New York Yankees in 1945, with the team winning 10 World Series during his ownership.
- Built the Flamingo Hotel in Las Vegas.

Running a successful business has a lot to do with integrity, work ethic, treating people fairly and kindly, and being honest in all your dealings.

—*Anne Beiler, founder, Auntie Anne's*

I believe in the supreme worth of the individual and in his right to life, liberty, and the pursuit of happiness.

—*John D. Rockefeller, billionaire, Standard Oil*

# Garrett Morgan

**High School Dropout**

## Words of Wisdom

Fame is a vapor, popularity an accident, and riches take wings. Only one thing endures and that is character.

—*Horace Greeley, founder, New York Tribune*

The fame you earn has a different taste from the fame that is forced upon you.

—*Gloria Vanderbilt, fashion designer*

## Innovators

- A son of former slaves, left home and school in his teens in search of employment in Cleveland, Ohio.
- Invented a protective hood for rescuers faced with smoke or chemical fumes.
- Saved the lives of 32 men who were trapped in a tunnel collapse under lake Erie in 1912, while wearing his safety hood.
- Started many businesses and patented several inventions, including a traffic signal.

My mother was the influence in my life. She was strong; she had great faith in the ultimate triumph of justice and hard work. She believed passionately in education.

—*John H. Johnson, founder,* Ebony Magazine

Clothes make the man. Naked people have little or no influence on society.

—*Mark Twain, author*

# Edwin Land

**College Dropout**

## Words of Wisdom

Always dream and shoot higher than you know you can do. Don't bother just to be better than your contemporaries or predecessors. Try to be better than yourself.

—*William Faulkner, author*

Success is ninety-nine percent failure.

—*Soichiro Honda, founder, Honda*

## Innovators

- Founded the Polaroid Company.
- Developed the Polaroid photography system, which allowed a person to take a picture on film and see the results within seconds.
- Dropped out of Harvard to develop this idea and to form a company selling it.
- As an American inventor, with over 500 patents, ranked behind only Nikola Tesla and Thomas Edison.

If we all worked on the assumption that what is accepted as true is really true, there would be little hope of advance.

—*Orville Wright, inventor*

And everything is possible, you've just got to find a way to make it work.

—*Wally Amos, founder, Famous Amos Cookies*

# Elijah McCoy

**High School Dropout**

## Words of Wisdom

I can think of nothing less pleasurable than a life devoted to pleasure.

—*John D Rockefeller, billionaire, Standard Oil*

Money doesn't change men, it merely unmasks them. If a man is naturally selfish or arrogant or greedy, the money brings that out, that's all.

—*Henry Ford, founder, Ford Motor Company*

## Innovators

- Was born to parents who escaped on the Underground Railroad.
- Received his first patent in 1872, for a automatic lubricator for the steam engines.
- Was a prolific inventor at the turn of 1900s.
- Received 57 patents for his inventions, which included a folding ironing board and a lawn sprinkler.

To succeed, one must be creative and persistent.
—*John H. Johnson, founder,* Ebony Magazine

The three great essentials to achieve anything worthwhile are: first, hard work; second, stick-to-itiveness; and third, common sense.
—*Thomas A. Edison, inventor*

# Florence Graham

**College Dropout**

## Words of Wisdom

I do not think there is any thrill that can go through the human heart like that felt by the inventor as he sees some creation of the brain unfolding to success. ... Such emotions make a man forget food, sleep, friends, love, everything.

—*Nikola Tesla, inventor*

## Innovators

- Opened her first salon in 1910 in a shop that had "Elizabeth" painted on half the window and kept it to save money, adding the name Arden from the title of a poem she had read, "Enoch Arden."
- Borrowed $6,000 from her brother to get her cosmetics business started and paid him back in full within six months.

What we do during our working hours determines what we have; what we do in our leisure hours determines what we are.

—*George Eastman, inventor*

You are ambitious, which, within reasonable bounds, does good rather than harm.

—*Abraham Lincoln, president*

# Bill Rosenberg

**Middle School Dropout**

## Words of Wisdom

A business absolutely devoted to service will have only one worry about profits. They will be embarrassingly large.
—*Henry Ford, founder, Ford Motor Company*

Frequently we live our lives on automatic pilot, taking each experience for granted.
—*Wally Amos, founder, Famous Amos Cookies*

## Innovators

- Dropped out of school during the Depression to help support his family.
- Founded Dunkin' Donuts in 1950.
- Went from five stores in 1954 to over 6,000 stories in 30 countries today.
- Founded the International Franchise Association in 1964, an organization that today has over 800 franchisors and more than 30,000 members.

All the adversity I've had in my life, all my troubles and obstacles, have strengthened me. ... You may not realize it when it happens, but a kick in the teeth may be the best thing in the world for you.

—*Walt Disney, founder, The Walt Disney Company*

Get your facts first, and then you can distort them as much as you please.

—*Mark Twain, author*

# David Neelman

**College Dropout**

## Words of Wisdom

Nobody can be successful unless he loves his work.
—*David Sarnoff, founder, NBC*

The Lord prefers common-looking people. That is why he makes so many of them.
—*Abraham Lincoln, president*

There is no such thing as a little freedom. Either you are all free, or you are not free.
—*Walter Cronkite, news anchor*

## Innovators

- Started his first discount travel business at age 23 and filed bankruptcy when he was 24.
- Founded Morris Air, a small discount commuter airline, 10 years later.
- Sold Morris Air to Southwest Airlines.
- Went to work at Southwest and was fired within five months.
- Founded JetBlue, the only challenger to Southwest, after his non-compete agreement with Southwest expired.

Failure is simply the opportunity to begin again, this time more intelligently.

*—Henry Ford, founder, Ford Motor Company*

One of the unfortunate things about our education system is that we do not teach students how to avail themselves of their subconscious capabilities.

*—Bill Lear, inventor*

# Frank Mars

**High School Dropout**

## Words of Wisdom

Harvard takes perfectly good plums as students and turns them into prunes.
—*Frank Lloyd Wright, architect*

In seeking truth you have to get both sides of a story.
—*Walter Cronkite, news anchor*

## Innovators

- Was so determined to make his candy company successful he neglected to feed his children, who were sent to live with their grandparents for fear of starving to death.
- Passed that trait on to one of those children, Forrest Mars, who did the same thing to his own children while adding to the Mars empire.
- Inspired one day while having a malted milk with Forrest, developed the Milky Way.
- Also developed Snickers and 3 Musketeers.

Crowded classrooms and half-day sessions
are a tragic waste of our greatest national resource,
the minds of our children.
— *Walt Disney, The Walt Disney Company*

If you have to have a job in this world,
a high-priced movie star is a pretty good gig.
— *Tom Hanks, actor*

# George Eastman

**High School Dropout**

## Words of Wisdom

All the people throughout my life who were naysayers pissed me off. But they've all given me a fervor, an angry ambition that cannot be stopped—and I look forward to finding a therapist and working on that.

—*Tobey Maguire, actor*

## Innovators

- Invented and patented a camera that used roll film.
- Founded Eastman Kodak.
- Gave generously during his life—over $100 million to universities and other charities.
- Said, "What we do during our working hours determines what we have; what we do in our leisure hours determines what we are."

We have our factory, which is called a stage. We make a product, we color it, we title it and we ship it out in cans.

—*Cary Grant, actor*

A word to the wise ain't necessary—it's the stupid ones that need the advice.

—*Bill Cosby, actor*

# Hiroshi Yamauchi

**College Dropout**

## Words of Wisdom

So never lose an opportunity of urging a practical beginning, however small, for it is wonderful how often in such matters the mustard-seed germinates and roots itself.

*—Florence Nightingale, nursing pioneer*

Thinking is the hardest work there is, which is probably the reason why so few engage in it.

*—Henry Ford, founder, Ford Motor Company*

## Innovators

- Took over his grandfather's trading card business.
- Introduced the most advanced video gaming console of its time, the Nintendo NES (Nintendo Entertainment System).
- Led Nintendo to develop over 250 games and sell over 2 billion copies of them.
- Stepped down as president in 2002 after leading the company for five decades.
- Is majority owner of the Seattle Mariners.

I don't know what I did in this life to deserve all of this. I'm just a girl from a trailer park who had a dream.

*—Hilary Swank, actress*

A man should never neglect his family for business.

*—Walt Disney, founder, The Walt Disney Company*

An investment in knowledge pays the best interest.

*—Benjamin Franklin, politician*

# Horace Greeley

**High School Dropout**

# Words of Wisdom

It has been my observation that most people get ahead during the time that others waste.

—*Henry Ford, founder, Ford Motor Company*

It is better to remain silent and be thought a fool than to speak out and remove all doubt.

—*Abraham Lincoln, president*

# Innovators

- Founded the *New York Tribune.*
- Assisted in the formation of the Republican party.
- Campaigned against slavery.
- Was elected to Congress in 1872.

Work and live to serve others, to leave the world a little better than you found it and garner
for yourself as much peace of mind as you can. This is happiness.

—*David Sarnoff, founder, NBC*

I only hope that we don't lose sight of one thing, that it was all started by a mouse.

—*Walt Disney, founder, The Walt Disney Company*

# Madame C.J. Walker

**Elementary School Dropout**

## Words of Wisdom

I thoroughly disapprove of duels. If a man should challenge me, I would take him kindly and forgivingly by the hand and lead him to a quiet place and kill him.

—*Mark Twain, author*

A penny saved is a penny earned.

—*Benjamin Franklin, politician*

## Innovators

- Was the first member of her family born free and was orphaned at 7, married at 14 and widowed at 20.
- Invented a line of hair care products while trying to treat her temporary baldness from a scalp ailment.
- Ran, by 1917, the largest company in the U.S. owned by an African American.
- Was the first female American millionaire.

Any fool can make things bigger, more complex and more violent. It takes a touch of genius—and a lot of courage—to move in the opposite direction.

—*Albert Einstein, physicist*

There's no reason to be the richest man in the cemetery. You can't do any business from there.

—*Colonel Sanders, founder, KFC*

# Frank Lloyd Wright

**College Dropout**

## Words of Wisdom

You spend so much time in your profession,
it ought to be something you love.

—*John H. Johnson, founder,* Ebony Magazine

Man is still the greatest miracle
and the greatest problem on this earth.

—*David Sarnoff, founder, NBC*

## Innovators

- Said, "Form and function should be one, joined in a spiritual union."
- Had an architectural career lasting 70 years.
- Designed 1,141 homes and buildings, of which 532 were completed before his death.
- Designed two of his most famous projects, the Guggenheim Museum and the Marin County Civic Center, during his final years.
- Was one of the most influential and imaginative architects of the twentieth century.

Anywhere I see suffering, that is where
I want to be, doing what I can.
—*Princess Diana, philanthropist*

If there are things you don't like in the world
you grew up in, make your own life different.
—*Dave Thomas, founder, Wendy's*

# Hans Christian Andersen

**High School Dropout**

## Words of Wisdom

Obstacles are those frightful things you see when you take your eyes off your goal.

— *Henry Ford, founder,* Ford Motor Company

Every day I run scared. That's the only way I can stay ahead.

— *John H. Johnson, founder,* Ebony Magazine

How very little can be done under the spirit of fear.

— *Florence Nightingale, nursing pioneer*

## Innovators

- Grew up in a one-room home in an impoverished family.
- Started working at age 11, when his father died, as a weaver's and then a tailor's apprentice.
- Failed as an actor, a poet, a novelist and a dramatist.
- Gained widespread acclaim during his lifetime for his many fairy tales, including "The Ugly Duckling," "The Emperor's New Clothes" and "The Princess and the Pea."

Memories of our lives, of our works and our deeds will continue in others.

—*Rosa Parks, human rights activist*

Opportunity is missed by most people because it is dressed in overalls and looks like work.

—*Thomas A. Edison, inventor*

# Richard Branson

**High School Dropout**

## Words of Wisdom

Our virtues and our failings are inseparable, like force and matter. When they separate, man is no more.

—*Nikola Tesla, inventor*

As I grow older, I pay less attention to what men say. I just watch what they do.

—*Andrew Carnegie, millionaire*

## Innovators

- Started a magazine while still in high school.
- Started his own record label, mobile phone service, airline, soft drink, and many other enterprises under the Virgin brand.
- Copiloted the first hot air balloon over the Atlantic Ocean.
- Set the record for flying a plane around the world.

A question that sometimes drives me hazy:
Am I—or are the others crazy?

—*Albert Einstein, physicist*

If my parents had discouraged me, I would have turned out very differently. They raised me in an open-minded, liberal environment.

—*Tom Ford, fashion designer*

# Bill Gates

**College Dropout**

## Words of Wisdom

We don't know a millionth of one percent about anything.

—*Thomas A. Edison, inventor*

Researchers have discovered that chocolate produces some of the same reactions in the brain as marijuana. The researchers also discovered other similarities between the two but can't remember what they are.

—*Matt Lauer, news anchor*

## Innovators

- Dropped out of Harvard.
- Cofounded Microsoft.
- Dominated personal computer software to become the richest person in the world.
- Has become a major philanthropist, with the Bill & Melinda Gates Foundation now world's largest charitable foundation.

My grandmother started walking five miles a day when she was sixty. She's ninety-seven now, and we don't know where the hell she is.

—*Ellen DeGeneres, comedian*

Do not squander time, for that is the stuff life is made of.

—*Benjamin Franklin, politician*

# John D. Rockefeller

**High School Dropout**

## Words of Wisdom

Surplus wealth is a sacred trust which its possessor is bound to administer in his lifetime for the good of the community.

—*Andrew Carnegie, millionaire*

To invent, you need a good imagination and a pile of junk.

—*Thomas A. Edison, inventor*

## Innovators

- Cofounded Standard Oil, at one point the largest oil company in the world.
- Became America's first billionaire.
- Was always a philanthropist, donating as a child and throughout his life to the Baptist church.
- Contributed significant amounts to many colleges in the Midwest and the South.
- Believed that "charity is injurious unless it helps the recipient to become independent of it."

With Malice toward none, with charity for all, with firmness in the right, as God gives us to see the right, let us strive on to finish the work we are in, to bind up the nation's wounds.

—*Abraham Lincoln, president*

You can do what you want to do. You can be what you want to be.

—*Dave Thomas, founders, Wendy's*

# Christopher Columbus

**High School Dropout**

## Words of Wisdom

Don't call me an icon. I'm just a mother trying to help.

—*Princess Diana, philanthropist*

The way to become rich is to put all your eggs in one basket and then watch that basket.

—*Andrew Carnegie, millionaire*

## Innovators

- Spent seven years seeking financial support from Spain for the voyage of 1492.
- Sailed into unknown waters, based on woefully inaccurate calculations of the Earth's circumference and with neither charts nor navigator, believing he was headed to Japan.
- Established the first modern shipping route across the Atlantic Ocean.
- Made a total of four voyages to the New World between 1492 and 1504.

Most folks are as happy as they make up their minds to be.

—*Abraham Lincoln, president*

Be not afraid of greatness: some are born great, some achieve greatness, and some have greatness thrust upon them.

—*William Shakespeare, playwright*

# Abraham Lincoln

**Elementary School Dropout**

## Words of Wisdom

Born of necessity, the little fellow [Mickey Mouse] literally freed us of immediate worry. He provided the means for expanding our organization to its present dimensions and for extending the medium of cartoon animation toward new entertainment levels. He spelled production liberation for us.

—*Walt Disney, founder, Walt The Disney Company*

## Innovators

- Lost his job in 1832.
- Failed in business in 1833.
- Suffered the death of his sweetheart in 1835.
- Was defeated for speaker of the Illinois assembly in 1838.
- Lost the nomination for Congress in 1843.
- Lost re-nomination in 1848.
- Was defeated for U.S. senate in 1854.
- Was defeated for nomination for V.P. in 1856.
- Was defeated for U.S. senate in 1858.
- Was elected president of the U.S. in 1860.

A man wrapped up in himself makes
 a very small bundle.

—*Benjamin Franklin, politician*

If you can do what you do best and be happy,
you're further along in life than most people.

—*Leonardo DiCaprio, actor*

# Benjamin Franklin

**High School Dropout**

## Words of Wisdom

Our greatest weakness lies in giving up. The most certain way to succeed is always to try just one more time.

—*Thomas A. Edison, inventor*

Nearly all men can stand adversity, but if you want to test a man's character, give him power.

—*Abraham Lincoln, president*

## Innovators

- Was the fifteenth of 17 children and a voracious reader as a child.
- Dropped out of Boston Latin School because of a shortage of funds for tuition.
- Helped write the Declaration of Independence, as a delegate from Pennsylvania.
- Gained prominence as an inventor, diplomat, scientist, composer, businessman, publisher, author and politician.
- Was the first U.S. Postmaster General.

To be a good actor you have to be something like a criminal, to be willing to break the rules to strive for something new.

—*Nicolas Cage, actor*

I had all the usual ambition growing up. I wanted to be a writer, a musician, a hockey player.
I wanted to do something that wasn't nine to five. Acting was the first thing I tried that clicked.

—*Michael J. Fox, actor*

# George Washington

**High School Dropout**

## Words of Wisdom

I steal from every movie ever made.
—*Quentin Tarantino, filmmaker*

I have been up against tough competition all my life. I wouldn't know how to get along without it.
—*Walt Disney, founder, The Walt Disney Company*

All I need is a camera and I'll make things happen.
—*Keenen Ivory Wayans, comedian*

## Innovators

- Was a surveyor, firefighter, battle-hardened soldier, and a plantation owner before the start of the American Revolution.
- Successfully led the fight for independence.
- Was the first to sign the U.S. Constitution.
- Established the national observance of Thanksgiving his first year as president, 1789.
- Retired as the first president after two terms, when there were 16 states in the union.

When you have a dream, you've got to grab it
and never let go.

—*Carol Burnett, comedian*

About the only problem with success is that
it does not teach you how to deal with failure.

—*Tommy Lasorda, baseball manager*

# Max Factor

**Elementary School Dropout**

## Words of Wisdom

An idea is salvation by imagination.
—*Frank Lloyd Wright, architect*

Every character I do is based on someone I know.
—*Tracey Ullman, actress*

## Innovators

- Was a makeup artist for the Russian royal ballet when, in 1904, at 27, he applied make up to his face to give the impression that he was sick, using this ruse to sneak out of the country with his wife and three children and escape to America.
- Set up shop in Los Angeles, California, selling cosmetics to the stars of early Hollywood.
- Was an innovator in the cosmetic industry, setting standards still practiced today.

The danger for children today, honey, is the news. Keep them away from news on television and you're going to have very, very fine, natural children.

—*Jerry Lewis, comedian*

If you have it and you know you have it, then you have it. If you have it and don't know you have it, you don't have it. If you don't have it but you think you have it, then you have it.

—*Jackie Gleason, comedian*

# Ole Kirk Christian

**Elementary School Dropout**

## Words of Wisdom

Giving birth is like taking your lower lip and forcing it over your head.

—*Carol Burnett, comedian*

I've always had a will to succeed, to win, however you phrase it.

—*Jack K. Cooke, billionaire, broadcasting*

## Innovators

- Was a carpenter who started a company in 1932 to make stepladders, wooden toys and other products.
- Named his company Lego, from the Danish words for "play well," in 1934.
- Lost the factory to fire in 1942.
- Introduced the precursor of today's Lego building blocks in 1949 and the modern design in 1958.
- Lost the factory to fire again in 1960 and finally stopped making wooden toys.

I have a policy that I get to spend as much on myself as I give away.

—*Jim Clark, billionaire, Netscape*

Guys ask me, don't I get burned out? How can you get burned out doing something you love? I ask you, have you ever got tired of kissing a pretty girl?

—*Tommy Lasorda, baseball manager*

# Jackie Cochran

**Elementary School Dropout**

## Words of Wisdom

And all people live, not by reason of any care they have for themselves, but by the love for them that is in other people.

—*Leo Tolstoy, author*

Either you think, or else others have to think for you and take power from you, pervert and discipline your natural tastes, civilize and sterilize you.

—*F. Scott Fitzgerald, playwright*

## Innovators

- Set more speed and altitude records than any of her contemporaries, male or female.
- Set a national air speed record from New York to Miami in 4 hours, 12 minutes, 27 seconds.
- Was the first woman to fly a bomber across the Atlantic Ocean.
- Was a successful entrepreneur in the cosmetics industry.

Just living is not enough. One must have sunshine, freedom and a little flower.

—*Hans Christian Andersen, author*

My life has been nothing but a failure.

—*Claude Monet, artist*

Study nature, love nature, stay close to nature. It will never fail you.

—*Frank Lloyd Wright, architect*

# Valentina Tereshkova

**High School Dropout**

## Words of Wisdom

You can think of Hollywood as high school. TV actors are freshmen, comedy actors are maybe juniors, and dramatic actors, they're the cool seniors.

—*Owen Wilson, actor*

You can't undo the past … but you can certainly not repeat it.

—*Bruce Willis, actor*

## Innovators

- Left school at 16 to work in a textile factory.
- Became the first woman in space at 26, as a Cosmonaut.
- Was the first woman to orbit the earth.
- Was the first woman to give birth after having visiting space.

Marriage is about the most expensive way for the average man to get laundry done.

—*Burt Reynolds, actor*

The simple act of paying attention can take you a long way.

—*Keanu Reeves, actor*

# Berry Gordy

**High School Dropout**

## Words of Wisdom

I am a blank slate, therefore I can create anything I want.

—*Tobey Maguire, actor*

From now on we live in a world where man has walked on the moon. It's not a miracle; we just decided to go.

—*Tom Hanks, actor*

## Innovators

- Dropped out of high school to become a boxer.
- Failed at his first business, 3-D Record Mart.
- Founded Motown Records.
- Discovered some of the biggest acts during the Sixties and Seventies, including the Jackson Five, Stevie Wonder, Gladys Knights, the Four Tops and the Temptations.
- Sold Motown Records in 1988 for $61 million.

Everyone wants to be Cary Grant.
Even I want to be Cary Grant.

*—Cary Grant, actor*

I love what I do. I take great pride in what I do. And I can't do something halfway, three-quarters, nine-tenths. If I'm going to do something, I go all the way.

*—Tom Cruise, actor*

# Frank Woodward

**High School Dropout**

## Words of Wisdom

The person who starts out simply with the idea of getting rich won't succeed; you must have a larger ambition. There is no mystery in business success. ... If you do each day's task successfully, and stay faithfully within these natural operations of commercial laws which I talk so much about, and keep your head clear, you will come out all right.

—*John D Rockefeller, billionaire, Standard Oil*

## Innovators

- Bought the rights to Jell-O for $450 when he was 20, after two other businessmen failed with the product.
- Had little success with Jell-O and was going to sell it to his plant supervisor for $35.
- Decided against that sale and was then able to build a multi-million dollar business within a few years.

Anyone can dabble, but once you've made that commitment, your blood has that particular thing in it, and it's very hard for people to stop you.

—*Bill Cosby, comedian*

When people don't believe in you, you have to believe in yourself.

—*Pierce Brosnan, actor*

# Henry Ford

**High School Dropout**

## Words of Wisdom

Things are never so bad they can't be made worse.
—*Humphrey Bogart, actor*

I've had great success being a total idiot.
—*Jerry Lewis, comedian*

## Innovators

- Left home at age 16 and took a job in a machine shop as an apprentice.
- Was working at the Edison Illuminating Company when he was 29.
- Developed his first automobile, called the Quadricycle, when he was 33.
- Failed with two other automobile companies before incorporating the Ford Motor Company in 1903, at 40.
- Dominated the industry by 1921, with a 55 percent market share.

I have never let my schooling interfere with my education.

—*Mark Twain, author*

Dreamers never die!

—*Woody Woodward, entrepreneur*

# William Lear

**High School Dropout**

## Words of Wisdom

While formal schooling is an important advantage, it is not a guarantee of success nor is its absence a fatal handicap.

— *Ray Kroc, billionaire, McDonald's Corporation*

Happiness is having a large, loving, caring, close-knit family in another city.

— *George Burns, comedian*

## Innovators

- Dropped out of school to join the Navy, where he became a pilot.
- Invented the first automotive eight track player.
- Received over 100 patents for his inventions in the aircraft and automotive industries.
- Developed the Learjet, still the premier private jet brand name.
- Was inducted in the International Aerospace Hall of Fame.

Genius is the ability to put into effect
what is on your mind.

*—F. Scott Fitzgerald, author*

A lifetime of happiness! No man alive could bear it; it would be hell on earth.

*—George Bernard Shaw, playwright*

Never confuse a single defeat with a final defeat.

*—F. Scott Fitzgerald, author*

# Nikola Tesla

**High School Dropout**

## Words of Wisdom

I confess that in 1901 I said to my brother Orville that man would not fly for fifty years.
—*Wilbur Wright, inventor*

Every man's life is a fairy tale written by God's fingers.
—*Hans Christian Andersen, author*

## Innovators

- Recognized for his advancements in Alternate Current. At the turn of the twentieth century Edison had America wired with Direct Current. It was Tesla's advancements in AC that allows current to flow longer distances than DC.
- The Supreme Court awarded Tesla the bragging rights of inventor of the radio a few months after is death in 1943.
- Tesla was awarded over 700 patents.

I have acted fearless and independent and I never will regret my course. I would rather be politically buried that to be hypocritically immortalized.

*—Davy Crockett, frontiersman*

Few are those who see with their own eyes and feel with their own hearts.

*—Albert Einstein, physicist*

# Florence Nightingale

**High School Dropout**

## Words of Wisdom

There is no substitute for hard work.
—*Thomas A. Edison, inventor*

Disneyland will never be completed. It will continue to grow as long as there is imagination left in the world.
—*Walt Disney, The Walt Disney Company*

## Innovators

- Was inspired to go into nursing, a field with a low reputation at the time, much against the wishes of her well-to-do parents.
- Successfully campaigned for improved conditions for the poor.
- Brought professional standards of care and hygiene to nursing and medical care under wartime conditions.
- Established the Nightingale Training School for nurses in London.
- Made major contributions to field of statistics.

To get an Oscar would be an incredible moment in my career, there is no doubt about that. But the *Lord of the Rings* films are not made for Oscars, they are made for the audience.

—*Peter Jackson, filmmaker*

The most important thing in acting is honesty. If you can fake that, you've got it made.

—*George Burns, comedian*

# William Shakespeare

**High School Dropout**

# Words of Wisdom

Be courageous! Have faith! Go Forward!
— *Thomas A. Edison, inventor*

## Innovators

- Was a successful actor before turning his hand to writing plays, at 26, to help keep his troupe supplied with scripts.
- Was considered good but not great during his lifetime.
- Wrote at least 37 plays and 154 sonnets, in addition to other poems.
- Remains the most quoted writer in English.
- Coined many words that remain part of the English language.

## Dropout Trivia

- The richest man in the world eleven years running, Bill Gates, with a net worth of $50 billion, is a dropout.
- Three of the ten richest people in the world are dropouts (number 1, Bill Gates; number 6, Paul Allen, worth $22 billion; number 10, Li Ka-shing, worth $18.8 billion).

## Dropout Trivia

- The richest man in the world eleven years running, Bill Gates, with a net worth of $50 billion, is a dropout.
- Three of the ten richest people in the world are dropouts (number 1, Bill Gates; number 6, Paul Allen, worth $22 billion; number 10, Li Ka-shing, worth $18.8 billion).

## Words of Wisdom

- The world's wealthiest high school dropout is Li Ka-shing.
- Four out of five of America's richest people are dropouts (number 1, Bill Gates; number 3, Paul Allen; number 4, Michael Dell, $17.1 billion; number 5, Sheldon Adelson, $6.1 billion).
- America's richest elementary school dropout, the late H.L. Hunt, was worth billions.
- America's richest high school dropout, J.R. Simplot, is worth $4.7 billion.

## Innovators

- The world's wealthiest high school dropout is Li Ka-shing.
- Four out of five of America's richest people are dropouts (number 1, Bill Gates; number 3, Paul Allen; number 4, Michael Dell, $17.1 billion; number 5, Sheldon Adelson, $6.1 billion).
- America's richest elementary school dropout, the late H.L. Hunt, was worth billions.
- America's richest high school dropout, J.R. Simplot, is worth $4.7 billion.

- America's richest college dropout is Bill Gates.
- Asia's richest resident, Li Ka-shing, is a high school dropout.
- Argentina's sole billionaire, Gregorio Perez, worth $1.7 billion, is a high school dropout.
- Spain's richest resident, Amancio Ortega, worth $14.8 billion, is a high school dropout.
- There are 68 billionaires who are dropouts and numerous millionaires.

# Words of Wisdom

- Many of the world's greatest inventions were developed by dropouts, including television, radio, airplanes, cars, motion pictures, the incandescent light bulb, the car stereo tape deck, the gas mask, the traffic signal, earmuffs, the game of basketball, the sewing machine—and many more.

# Innovators

- Many of the world's greatest inventions were developed by dropouts, including television, radio, airplanes, cars, motion pictures, the incandescent light bulb, the car stereo tape deck, the gas mask, the traffic signal, earmuffs, the game of basketball, the sewing machine—and many more.

- Some of history's greatest companies were founded by dropouts, including Kodak, Polaroid, Famous Amos, Disney, Ford, Learjet, Bank of America, Motown Records, Whole Foods, Domino's, Apple Computer, Netscape, Microsoft, Polo, Jet Blue, Dunkin' Donuts, NBC, KFC, Wendy's, McDonald's, Holiday Inn and Rolling Stone Magazine.

## Words of Wisdom

- Titanic, the highest grossing movie of all time was directed by a dropout (James Cameron); and the two lead actors were dropouts (Leonardo Di Caprio and Kate Winslet)
- Some of the highest-paid actors in the world (Tom Cruise, Tom Hanks, Jim Carrey, Johnny Depp and Leonardo Di Caprio) are all dropouts.

## Innovators

- Titanic, the highest grossing movie of all time was directed by a dropout (James Cameron); and the two lead actors were dropouts (Leonardo Di Caprio and Kate Winslet)
- Some of the highest-paid actors in the world (Tom Cruise, Tom Hanks, Jim Carrey, Johnny Depp and Leonardo Di Caprio) are all dropouts.

- A member of the all-time top selling band The Beatles, George Harrison, was a dropout.
- Some of the highest-paid actresses in the world (Cameron Diaz, Nicole Kidman, Angelina Jolie and Drew Barrymore) are all dropouts.
- The U.S. penny and quarter-dollar coins, as well as the one, five, twenty, one hundred and thousand-dollar bills all have images of dropouts.

## Words of Wisdom

- "I have watched all the dropouts who made their own rules" is a line in Ozzy Osbourne's song, "Crazy Train." Ozzy is a high school dropout as is his daughter.
- One of the top-grossing films of 2005, *War of the Worlds*, was written by a dropout (H.G. Wells), was directed by a dropout (Steven Spielberg) and starred a dropout (Tom Cruise).

## Innovators

- "I have watched all the dropouts who made their own rules" is a line in Ozzy Osbourne's song, "Crazy Train." Ozzy is a high school dropout as is his daughter.
- One of the top-grossing films of 2005, *War of the Worlds*, was written by a dropout (H.G. Wells), was directed by a dropout (Steven Spielberg) and starred a dropout (Tom Cruise).

- Elijah McCoy, who invented the ironing board as well as a lubrication system for steam engines, was a dropout. He attracted notice among his African-American contemporaries. Booker T. Washington in *Story of the Negro* (1909) recognized him as having produced more patents than any other African-American inventor up to that time.

# Words of Wisdom

- Madame C.J. Walker, the first African-American millionaire, was a dropout.
- America's first millionaire, John Jacob Astor, was high school dropout.
- America's first billionaire, John D Rockefeller Sr., was high school dropout.

# Innovators

- Madame C.J. Walker, the first African-American millionaire, was a dropout.
- America's first millionaire, John Jacob Astor, was high school dropout.
- America's first billionaire, John D Rockefeller Sr., was high school dropout.

## About the Author

Woody Woodward dropped out of high school at 16, was a millionaire at 26, and was broke by 27. Within five years of being nearly bankrupt, he built from scratch a $30 million mortgage and real estate firm. Not only has he made more than his money back, he has gone on to become an author of seven books, a professional speaker and an investor. He lives in southern California with his wife and three children.

# Words of Wisdom

## Contribute a Story to Millionaire Dropouts

Go to www.MillionaireDropouts.com and add a famous dropout. We are always looking for inspiring stories of those who beat the odds and overcame obstacles.

---

# Innovators

## Contribute a Story to Millionaire Dropouts

Go to www.MillionaireDropouts.com and add a famous dropout. We are always looking for inspiring stories of those who beat the odds and overcame obstacles.

## Give the gift of Millionaire Dropouts™ to your friends, family and business associates

| | |
|---|---:|
| *Millionaire Dropouts: Inspiring Stories of the World's Most Successful Failures* | $16.95 |
| *Millionaire Dropouts High School Edition: Never Let Your Schooling Interfere with Your Education* | $12.95 |
| *Millionaire Dropouts College Edition: Why Dropping Out Might Be the Best Decision You Ever Made* | $14.95 |
| *Millionaire Dropouts Parents Edition: Why You Should Support Your Child Who Wants to Drop Out* | $16.95 |
| *Millionaire Dropouts Biography Edition: Biographies of the World's Most Successful Failures* | $16.95 |
| *Millionaire Dropouts Mini-Book: Words of Wisdom* | $6.95 |
| *Millionaire Dropouts Mini-Book: Innovators* | $6.95 |

Order online at www.MillionaireDropouts.com

## Give the gift of Millionaire Dropouts™ to your friends, family and business associates

| | |
|---|---:|
| *Millionaire Dropouts: Inspiring Stories of the World's Most Successful Failures* | $16.95 |
| *Millionaire Dropouts High School Edition: Never Let Your Schooling Interfere with Your Education* | $12.95 |
| *Millionaire Dropouts College Edition: Why Dropping Out Might Be the Best Decision You Ever Made* | $14.95 |
| *Millionaire Dropouts Parents Edition: Why You Should Support Your Child Who Wants to Drop Out* | $16.95 |
| *Millionaire Dropouts Biography Edition: Biographies of the World's Most Successful Failures* | $16.95 |
| *Millionaire Dropouts Mini-Book: Words of Wisdom* | $6.95 |
| *Millionaire Dropouts Mini-Book: Innovators* | $6.95 |

Order online at www.MillionaireDropouts.com

www.ingramcontent.com/pod-product-compliance
Lightning Source LLC
LaVergne TN
LVHW091552060526
838200LV00036B/803